Barbie™

Fun to Cook

DK

A Dorling Kindersley Book

Dorling **DK** Kindersley
LONDON, NEW YORK, SYDNEY, DELHI,
PARIS, MUNICH, and JOHANNESBURG

Written and edited by Fiona Munro
Art Editor Goldy Broad
Art Director Cathy Tincknell
Publishing Manager Cynthia O'Neill
Associate Designers Jane Thomas, Laia Roses
Photography Dave King
Home Economist Katharine Ibbs
Production Nicola Torode
DTP Design Andrew O'Brien

Barbie photography by Tom Wolfson, Laura Lynch,
Mark Adams, Judy Tsuno and the Mattel Photo Studio

First American Edition, 2001
00 01 02 03 04 05 10 9 8 7 6 5 4 3 2 1
Published in the United States by Dorling Kindersley
Publishing, Inc., 95 Madison Avenue, New York, NY 10016

Library of Congress Cataloging-in-Publication Data
Barbie fun to cook book.-- 1st American ed.
    p. cm.
    ISBN 0-7894-7335-6
    1. Cookery–Juvenile literature. [1. Cookery.] I. Title:
Fun to cook book. II. DK Publishing, Inc.
TX652.5 .B219 2001
641.5'123--dc21
    00-064338

Color reproduction by Media Development
Printed and bound in Italy by L.E.G.O

Dorling Kindersley would like to thank the following for
appearing in this book: Polly Broad, Jake Davies, Jordan
Davis, Alexandra Hayes, Harriet Hunter, Jasmine Marsh,
Nicola Mooi, Demi Ryan, Jordann Sewell, Savina and Shirine
Shah, Hannah Shone, Shianne St Louis.

Dorling Kindersley would also like to
thank Kitschen Sync for loan of props.

see our complete
catalog at
www.dk.com

Contents

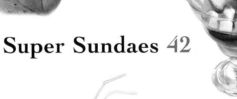

Getting Ready to Cook!

I love cooking and it's easy when you know how! For each recipe inside, there are pictures of all the things you will need, from ingredients to kitchen tools as well as clear step-by-step guides to follow. Don't forget to ask an adult to help whenever you see the (!) symbol. Let's start!

Kitchen rules

It's important to follow these rules, every time you cook.

1 Be careful with sharp knives. Use a chopping board and keep fingers away from the blade.

2 Wear oven mitts to protect your hands if picking up hot things or using the oven or stovetop.

3 When you are using the top of the stove, turn the saucepan handles to the side, so you do not knock them over.

4 When you take hot things out of the oven, put them on a wooden board, not straight onto the work surface.

5 Always wear an apron, tie back long hair, and wash your hands.

6 Read the recipe carefully and check you have all the things you need.

7 Collect the ingredients you will need. Measure them carefully.

Tips on how to use this book:

If using the oven or broiler, look here to find the temperature. Remember to turn the oven or broiler on 20 minutes before you need them (preheating).

Words in *italic* type are explained more fully on page 48.

Look at this part of the page to find out how long the recipe will take to make.

Set the oven to 350°F/180°C

20 minutes to make ♥ 15 minutes to bake ♥ LUNCHBOX IDEAS

Chunky Chocolate Cookies

If you really love chocolate then these cookies are just the treat for you! They are made with great big chunks of chocolate so they taste extra yummy. Take plenty to school in your lunchbox, because all your friends are sure to want one!

To make about 20 cookies you will need . . .

Mmm, chocolate!

1 egg, *beaten*

8 tablespoons/ 100 g softened butter

1½ cups/ 150 g all-purpose flour

⅓ cup/75 g light brown sugar

¼ cup/50 g sugar

½ teaspoon salt

½ teaspoon baking soda

6 oz/150 g good quality semisweet chocolate

½ teaspoon vanilla flavoring

Cook's tools

Chopping board

Baking sheet

Wire cooling rack

Wooden spoon

Palette knife

Wax paper

Scissors

Rolling pin

Large mixing bowl

Plastic bag (like a freezer bag)

2 teaspoons

1 Preheat the oven. Break chocolate into squares and put into plastic bag. Place on a solid surface.

2 With a rolling pin, break the chocolate into chunks. Keep your fingers out of the way!

3 In a bowl, *beat* butter with all the sugar until creamy and smooth. Gradually *beat* in egg.

4 *Beat* in flour, salt, vanilla, and baking soda. Stir in the chocolate chunks.

5 Spoon mounds onto a baking sheet lined with wax paper. Leave plenty of space around each one.

6 Bake for 10-15 minutes or until golden. Take out of the oven and leave on the pan for five minutes to harden before moving to a wire rack to cool.

Great big chunks of chocolate!

Barbie says:
Try making these cookies with chunks of white or milk chocolate, too!

16

17

Quantities for each recipe are shown in both standard and metric measurements. Make sure you stick to using one set or the other, don't mix them up.

Each recipe includes a tip from Barbie. This might be a helpful hint or a suggestion on how to vary the taste or ingredients.

Look out for this symbol. It means you should ask an adult to help you with this part of the recipe.

A Fruity Feast

Here are two ideas for a fabulously fruity brunchtime treat, each using almost the same ingredients! Choose between a cool smoothie and a beautiful salad for a healthy, colorful kick-start to the day!

For a smoothie or a salad you will need . . .

Pineapple Juice

8 large strawberries

1 ripe banana

3½ oz/100 ml pineapple juice for a smoothie OR 2 tablespoons pineapple chunks for a salad.

1 tablespoon honey

3 tablespoons plain yogurt

Cook's tools

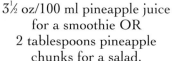

Tablespoon

Chopping board   Large glass   Blender   Sharp knife

1 To make a smoothie or a salad, first use a sharp knife to cut all the fruit up into chunks.

2 To make a salad, mix the yogurt with the honey, and layer with fruit in a glass. Serve.

1 To make a smoothie, put the fruit chunks, pineapple juice, yogurt, and honey into a blender. Put the lid on firmly.

2 Now *blend* until the mixture is smooth and pour into a large glass. Drink right away!

Fresh, fruity fun!

You could decorate your salad with a tablespoon of granola or nuts.

Sunshine Breakfast

Make this as a surprise for a special friend on her birthday, or on Mother's Day to show your mom how much you love her. It would make a lovely sunny surprise on a cold winter's day, too! Sometimes I just make it for myself though — I love to dip the toasty fingers into the creamy egg yolk. Mmm!

You will need . . .

2 slices of bread   ½ teaspoon butter   1 egg

Cook's tools

Large cookie cutter

Small bowl

Sharp knife

Chopping board

Non-stick frying pan   Ramekin   Pancake turner

Barbie says:
When cooking your egg, keep the heat low so you don't burn the toast!

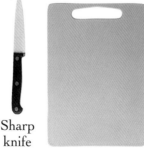

1 Use a bowl or saucer to cut a large circle from one slice of bread. With a cookie cutter, cut out a smaller circle inside.

Sunny side up!

2 Remove crusts from second slice of bread and cut into finger shapes.

Make sure the hole you make in the bread is big enough for the egg!

3 Melt the butter in a frying pan over a low heat. Fry the bread, turning over when golden.

4 Break the egg into a ramekin, then tip into hole in the bread. Fry gently until egg is cooked.

Lovely crunchy fingers – perfect for dipping!

Mini Muffins

Everybody loves muffins!
Now you can impress your friends
and family by making delicious
fruity muffins yourself. They are so
easy and quick to make, soon you
will be experimenting with different
flavors! Muffins taste great eaten
warm from the oven, maybe with
butter or a spoonful of sour cream.

To make about 20 you will need . . .

4 tablespoons/
50 g butter

⅔ cup/150 ml
milk

2 cups/200 g
all-purpose
flour

¾ cup/150 g
sugar

2 teaspoons
baking powder

½ teaspoon
salt

1 egg, *beaten*

4 oz/100 g blueberries or raspberries

Cook's tools

Large mixing bowl

Saucepan

Sieve

Measuring
cup

Two
teaspoons

Wooden spoon

Paper liners

2 x 12 hole
muffin pans

Wire cooling rack

Barbie says:

When your muffins
are cooked, leave them
in the pan to cool
down a little so you
don't burn yourself!

1 Preheat the oven. Melt
butter in pan over a low
heat. Remove from stove
and stir in milk and egg.

2 *Sift* flour, baking
powder, and salt into
a mixing bowl. Stir in the
sugar and fruit.

3 Carefully add melted butter, milk, and egg mixture to the flour, sugar, and fruit mixture.

4 Now mix everything together quickly and gently. Don't worry if the mixture looks lumpy.

5 Using two teaspoons, transfer the mixture to muffin pans that you have lined with paper liners.

Yum, what fun!

6 Bake for about 20 minutes or until golden and well risen. Allow to cool in tin, then move to a wire rack.

Sandwich Stack

One of these fabulous sandwiches is just what you need in your lunchbox to keep you going during a busy day! As well as trying the ideas below, experiment with different breads such as wholewheat or rye. The fillings taste great on crackers, too!

You will need . . .

For a Turkey and Tomato Sub:

3 slices of tomato

1 submarine roll

2 or 3 slices of turkey

Mayo

1 tablespoon mayonnaise

2 or 3 lettuce leaves

2 or 3 slices of cheese

For a Tuna Pita Pocket:

1 pita pocket

1 teaspoon capers

2 tablespoons canned kidney beans

Tuna

3 tablespoons canned tuna fish

Corn

1 tablespoon canned corn

For a Cream Cheese and Nut Life Preserver:

1 bagel

1 tablespoon raisins

1 apple, cored and *chopped*

Cream Cheese

1 tablespoon *chopped* nuts

2 tablespoons cream cheese

For a Mexican Wrap:

Sour Cream

1 flour tortilla

6 to 8 strips of pepper (any)

1 tablespoon sour cream

2 or 3 lettuce leaves

1 teaspoon black or green olives, sliced

Cook's tools

Sharp knife

Table knife

Tablespoon

Teaspoon

Small mixing bowl

Toothpicks (optional)

Chopping board

Barbie says:
Knives can be dangerous. Ask an adult to help you cut bread.

Turkey and Tomato Sub

Spread the bottom of your sub with mayonnaise

Layer the lettuce, turkey, tomato, and cheese inside

Tuna Pita Pocket

Mix all ingredients together and fill pocket!

Can't wait 'til lunch time!

Cream Cheese and Nut Life Preserver

Using a toothpick to hold your wrap together looks very stylish, but take it out before you start to eat!

Mexican Wrap

Layer lettuce, pepper, and olive slices along the middle of the flat tortilla

Mix all ingredients together and spoon onto bagel

Top with sour cream. Roll over one edge, then the other. Cut in half.

13

Favorite Aprinana Cake

Apricots and bananas taste really great together! I like to bake this cake on the weekend and put slices in Skipper's lunchbox for her to share with friends at school. It's full of good things, and will fill you up until suppertime!

Barbie says:
Try using some *chopped* nuts or dried cranberries instead of apricots!

You will need . . .

8 tablespoons/100 g butter

2 eggs, *beaten*

A little oil for greasing

2 cups/200 g all-purpose flour

1 cup/100 g light brown sugar (plus 2 tablespoons for topping – optional)

Zest of ½ a lemon

1 teaspoon baking powder

½ teaspoon salt

2 oz/50 g dried apricots, *chopped*

3 ripe bananas, crushed

For the topping (optional):

Handful of dried banana slices

2 tablespoons honey

Cook's tools

An 8 x 4 x 3 inch loaf pan

Wax paper

Scissors

Wire cooling rack

Chopping board

Sieve

Tablespoon

Large mixing bowl

Wooden spoon

Sharp knife

Grater

Brush

1 Preheat oven. Grease pan and line with a strip of wax paper the same width but twice the length of pan.

2 Put butter, sugar, and zest (see tip box on page 20) into a bowl and *beat* well. Gradually *beat* in eggs.

3 *Sift* the flour, baking powder, and salt into the mixture. *Beat* well. Stir in the apricots and bananas. Spoon into pan. Bake for one hour.

4 For topping: at the end of cooking time, spoon the honey over the cake, and scatter over dried bananas. Sprinkle with brown sugar and cook for another ten minutes.

5 Remove from oven and leave to cool in pan for ten minutes. Now, hold the ends of the paper and move cake to wire rack until cold.

Chunky Chocolate Cookies

If you really love chocolate then these cookies are just the treat for you! They are made with great big chunks of chocolate so they taste extra yummy. Take plenty to school in your lunchbox, because all your friends are sure to want one!

To make about 20 cookies you will need . . .

1 egg,
beaten

8 tablespoons/
100 g softened
butter

1½ cups/150 g
all-purpose
flour

⅓ cup/75 g
light brown
sugar

¼ cup/50 g
sugar

½ teaspoon
salt

½ teaspoon
baking soda

6 oz/150 g good quality
semisweet chocolate

½ teaspoon
vanilla flavoring

Mmm, chocolate!

Cook's tools

Chopping board

Baking sheet

Wire cooling rack

Wooden spoon

Palette
knife

Scissors

Wax paper

Rolling pin

Large mixing
bowl

Plastic bag
(like a freezer bag)

2 teaspoons

1 Preheat the oven. Break chocolate into squares and put into plastic bag. Place on a solid surface.

2 With a rolling pin, break the chocolate into chunks. Keep your fingers out of the way!

3 In a bowl, *beat* butter with all the sugar until creamy and smooth. Gradually *beat* in egg.

4 *Beat* in flour, salt, vanilla, and baking soda. Now stir in chocolate chunks.

5 Spoon mounds onto a baking sheet lined with wax paper. Leave plenty of space around each one.

6 Bake for 10-15 minutes or until golden. Take out of the oven and leave on the pan for five minutes to harden, before moving to a wire rack to cool.

Great big chunks of chocolate!

Barbie says:
Try making these cookies with chunks of white or milk chocolate too!

17

Fruity Freezies

Have some of these in the freezer during the hot summer months for a cool after-school treat! They are easy to make but remember they will take a few hours to freeze before you can enjoy them! Creamy Freezies taste great with raspberry or banana yogurt, too. And try Chewy Freezies with pineapple or cranberry juice.

For 2 of each Freezie you will need . . .

For Chewy Freezies

Orange juice

Handful of fruity jelly beans

For Creamy Freezies

2 x 6 oz cartons of strawberry yogurt

8 strawberries

Barbie says:
Make pretty Freezies to serve at a party! They are a special treat that can be made well in advance!

Cook's tools

2 plastic cups or yogurt containers

Chopping board

Teaspoon

Sharp knife

2 plastic teaspoons or wooden Popsicle sticks

Chewy Freezies

1 Line the bottom of each cup with a variety of your favorite colorful jelly beans.

2 Half-fill with orange juice. Freeze for one hour or until slushy. Stand sticks or spoons in center.

3 Pop the Freezies back into the freezer for three hours. Remove cups and eat right away!

Creamy Freezies

1 Slice the strawberries. Layer in cups with the yogurt, tucking some slices down the sides.

2 Freeze for one hour or until slushy. Stand the sticks or spoons in the center. Freeze again.

3 The Freezies should be frozen after three hours. Remove cups and eat before they melt!

They're so Cool!

Lemon Cooler and Super Shakes

Here are two great ideas for sophisticated drinks. Lemon Cooler is delicious when you're really thirsty, while a Super Shake is rich and smooth, perfect for more dreamy-creamy days. Dilute the Lemon Cooler before you drink it, but gulp your shake straight up and right away!

You will need . . .

For Lemon Cooler:

Zest of
1 lemon

1¼ cups/
350 mls water

Juice of
8 lemons

2 cups/350 g
sugar

Barbie says:
For lemon zest, grate just the colored part of the skin on the finest part of a grater.

For 1 Super Shake:

1 tablespoon
vanilla ice
cream

⅔ cup/
150 ml milk

3 tablespoons
plain yogurt

1 tablespoon
honey

For a blueberry shake add:

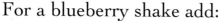

3 oz/75 g blueberries

For a banana shake add:

1 ripe banana,
cut into chunks

For a chocolate shake add:

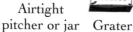

1 heaped tablespoon chocolate drink mix

Cook's tools

For the Lemon Cooler:

Wooden spoon

Airtight
pitcher or jar

Grater

Measuring
cup

Large
saucepan

For a Super Shake:

Table
knife

A tall
glass

Blender

For the Lemon Cooler:

1 Put sugar, water, and lemon zest into a large saucepan. Stir over a low heat until sugar has melted.

2 Turn up heat and bring to a *boil*. Stir for five minutes then remove from heat and let it cool.

3 When mixture is almost cold, add the lemon juice, pour into an airtight jar, and chill.

For a Super Shake:

1 Put banana, blueberries, or chocolate drink mix into blender with other ingredients and *blend* until smooth.

Pour Lemon Cooler over ice and dilute (approx 1 part Cooler to 5 parts water)

For an extra cool treat, put your glass in the freezer for ten minutes before pouring in the shake!

Blueberry Super Shake

Rainbow Snack Sticks

You can make a Snack Stick with anything that will fix on a skewer! Try crunchy vegetables, tasty fruit, or even chewy sweet treats! They look so pretty and the tasty dips make them even more tempting. Let your friends choose their favorite things to eat, and make their own colorful Snack Stick!

You could use . . .

Basil leaves

Hard cheese

Asparagus, cooked

Peppers

Cherry tomatoes

Pepperoni slices

Shrimp, cooked

Cocktail franks or sliced large ones

Mozzarella cheese

Olives, pitted

Mango

Strawberries

Marshmallows

Chewy sweets

Fudge

Banana

Chunks of canteloupe

Cook's tools

Chopping board

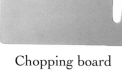
Wooden skewers

Sharp knife

Tablespoon

Small mixing bowl

Cookie cutters

For the sweet dip:

Handful of mini marshmallows

1 tablespoon powdered sugar

8 oz/200 g cream cheese

Juice of 1 orange

For the savory dip:

2 slices of bacon, grilled and crumbled

2 tablespoons mayonnaise

1 tablespoon sour cream

1 tomato, seeded and *chopped*

22

1 Choose foods that will look and taste good together. Then cut them into chunks or shapes.

2 Now thread everything onto skewers. Combine them in a way that shows off colors and textures.

3 Make dip by mixing either all the savory ingredients together or all the sweet ones.

Looks like fun!

Try this for delicious savory dipping!

These bite-sized hot dogs taste great with crunchy pepper strips

Use cookie cutters to make great shapes from mozzarella cheese

This pretty dip is as sweet as you!

Make a traffic light stick from three types of canteloupe

For a very special snack, try shrimp, asparagus, and mango

Barbie says:
Skewers are sharp. It's best to take your snacks off their sticks before you eat them!

Cute Cookies

Aren't these the prettiest cookies you've ever seen? They are perfect for a party and lots of fun to make. I have made a bouquet of flowers, but you could use any shaped cookie cutters. Decorating them is the best part — invite some friends over to help!

Use a spatula to spread the icing

To make about 20 cookies you will need . . .

For the icing you will need:

2 cups/200 g all-purpose flour

50 g/2 oz sugar

Pinch of salt

8 tablespoons/ 100 g softened butter

1 egg, *beaten*

 Drop of vanilla flavoring

2 cups/200 g powdered sugar

Warm water

 Food coloring

Cook's tools

Fork

Teaspoon

Wire cooling rack

Large mixing bowl

Rolling pin

Wax paper

Sieve

Cookie cutters

Baking sheet

Colored sugar crystals look great!

For the icing you will need:

Medium mixing bowl

Wooden spoon

Scissors

Spatula

Toothpicks

Barbie says:
Try lemon or orange cookies — add a pinch of lemon or orange zest to the mixture (see tip on page 20).

1 Preheat the oven. *Sift* flour into a bowl. Add butter and *rub in* flour until mixture looks like fine breadcrumbs.

2 Stir in the sugar. Add the egg, a little at a time, stirring with a fork until the mixture sticks together.

3 Gather the mixture together and place on a floured surface. Sprinkle a little flour onto your rolling pin, too.

Use candies or colored sprinkles as decorations

4 Roll out to ¼ inch/5 mm thick and cut out shapes. Transfer to a baking sheet lined with wax paper.

5 Bake for 20-25 minutes. Remove from oven and, after five minutes, move to a wire rack until cold.

You could arrange green ribbon between your cookies to make a bouquet

Now make the icing...

Oh, so pretty!

1 *Sift* the powdered sugar into a bowl. Stir in water, a little at a time, to make a thick paste.

2 Add drops of food coloring, using a toothpick, until you have just the right color.

Beautiful Birthday Cake

Birthdays are a time for parties, and this is the perfect cake for a celebration! Icing and decorating it is lots of fun — let your imagination run free! Your cake will look so pretty you won't want to eat it, but luckily it tastes just as good as it looks!

You will need . . .

For the cake:

¾ cup/150 g softened butter or margarine

3 tablespoons strawberry or raspberry jam

3 drops vanilla flavoring

¾ cup/150 g self-rising flour, *sifted*

Sugar

¾ cup/ 150 g sugar

2 tablespoons warm water

Baking Powder

1 teaspoon baking powder

3 eggs, *beaten*

A little oil for greasing

For the icing:

Powdered Sugar

1½ cups/ 150 g powdered sugar, *sifted*

Red food coloring

Warm water

To decorate:

Colored sprinkles

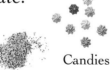

Candies

Cook's tools

Sieve

Large mixing bowl   Small mixing bowl

Wooden spoon

Wax paper

Brush

Tablespoon

Wire cooling rack

Scissors

2 x 8 inch round cake pans

Spatula

Pencil

Barbie says:
If the cake mixture is too thick at stage 3, add a teaspoon of water and beat again.

1 Preheat oven. Grease pans. On wax paper, use the base of one pan to draw two circles. Cut out and place one in each pan.

2 Put all the cake ingredients (except the jam) in a large mixing bowl. *Beat* well with a wooden spoon.

3 When your mixture drops easily from the spoon, put half in the bottom of each pan. Level out the mixture.

4 Bake for 25 minutes or until cakes feel firm in the center and are golden brown.

5 Cool for five minutes, then slide knife around edges and move cakes to wire rack. Remove paper.

Birthday girl!

You can buy icing in tubes to make flowers

Use a spatula to spread the icing

You could color ready-made icing and cut out shapes with cookie cutters

6 In a small bowl, stir jam to soften. When the cakes are cold, spread half on bottom of each.

Now make the icing on page 24 and decorate your cake.

Sweet Dreams

You and your friends can have so much fun making these delicious treats! Nuts and fruit are good for you — and they taste great. For something extra-special why not try dipping little cookies or marshmallows into creamy white chocolate? Arrange your Sweet Dreams beautifully, so they look just as dreamy as they taste!

You could use . . .

4 oz/100 g milk or semisweet chocolate

Dried apricots

Cherries

Strawberries

Little cookies

Marshmallows

Chopped nuts

Brazil nuts

Colored sprinkles

Cook's tools

Wax paper

Large ovenproof bowl

Scissors

Baking sheet

Small saucepan

Wooden spoon

Barbie says:
For melted chocolate that is smooth and shiny, keep the heat low and try not to stir!

1 Break the chocolate into the ovenproof bowl. Small chunks will melt more easily.

2 Rest the bowl on top of a pan of *simmering* water (don't let it actually touch the water).

3 When the chocolate has melted, take the bowl off the heat, and stir gently once or twice.

4 Dip fruit, nuts, etc., halfway into chocolate and then into chopped nuts or sprinkles.

5 Lay Sweet Dreams on a baking sheet lined with wax paper. Leave to set in a cool place – but not the fridge – for an hour before taking off the wax paper and serving.

Wrap your Sweet Dreams in pretty paper and give them away as presents or party favors.

As sweet as you are!

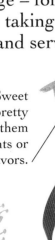

Pick-up Pizzas

Everybody loves pizza! There are so many different toppings to try, and I love to test out new flavors on my friends. For a special occasion it's fun to make lots of different ones — they look so colorful and taste just great!

For 10 you will need . . .

For the crust:

½ teaspoon mustard

½ teaspoon baking powder

½ teaspoon paprika

¼ teaspoon salt

1 cup/100 g self-rising flour

1 oz/25 g Cheddar cheese, grated

1 egg, *beaten*

2 tablespoons/ 25 g softened butter

1 tablespoon milk

For the tomato sauce:

1 tablespoon/ 12 g butter

½ teaspoon sugar

½ an onion, *chopped* finely

½ a 14oz/400g can *chopped* tomatoes

1 teaspoon tomato purée

Ides for toppings:

Mozzarella cheese

Peppers, sliced

Olives, sliced

Mushrooms, sliced

Canned corn

Asparagus, cooked

Pepperoni slices

Pineapple chunks

Ham, sliced

Red onion slices

3 oz/75 g Cheddar cheese, grated

Cook's tools

Grater

Large mixing bowl

Wax paper

Wooden spoon

Baking sheet

Rolling pin

Teaspoon

Saucepan

Spatula

Fork

Chopping board

Scissors

Sharp knife

1 Preheat the oven. Put the crust ingredients in a bowl and *beat* well to form a dough.

2 Place dough on a floured surface. Divide into ten pieces. Roll each into a ball, then flatten.

Now make the tomato sauce:

3 Place rounds on a baking sheet lined with wax paper. Prick each crust with a fork.

4 Melt butter in a pan and cook onions until soft. Add all the other ingredients and *simmer*.

5 When the sauce has thickened, after about ten minutes, spread a little on each crust.

Now put the pizzas together:

6 Now lay on your choice of toppings, sprinkle on the cheese, and bake for 20 minutes until golden and bubbling.

Say "cheese"!

Don't spread topping right to the edge of your pizza crust. If you leave a little gap they are easier to pick up!

Barbie says:
Use cookie cutters to make shapes from cheese and ham, then decorate your pizzas!

Burger Bites

These burgers taste great! With this recipe you can make eight mini burgers or four big burgers for really hungry family and friends! Try serving them in dinner rolls or pita pockets for a change, with a fresh green salad. Don't forget the ketchup!

You will need . . .

4 or 8 burger buns, dinner rolls, or pita pockets

½ teaspoon mustard

1 lb/450 g lean ground beef

Black pepper

½ teaspoon salt

½ teaspoon Worcestershire Sauce

½ an onion

1 egg yolk

1 cup/50 g fresh breadcrumbs

Serve your burgers with any of the following to make them extra tasty:

Slices of cheese

Lettuce leaves

Slices of cucumber

Slices of tomato

Red onion rings

Mayonnaise   Ketchup

Cook's tools

Chopping board

Large mixing bowl

Sharp knife

Fork   Spatula

1 Peel the onion and *chop* finely using a sharp knife. Transfer to a large mixing bowl.

2 Add ground beef, egg yolk, breadcrumbs, mustard, Worcester sauce, salt, and pepper. Mix well.

3 Heat up grill. Divide mixture into either four or eight. Roll into balls and flatten with a fork.

4 Lift your burgers onto grill pan of your stove or outdoor grill with a spatula or pancake turner.

5 Cook each side for five to ten minutes, or until firm and brown. Larger burgers will take longer.

Burgers are brilliant!

You could serve homemade salsa with your burgers (see page 40)

For a spicy burger, stir a few drops of chili sauce into mayonnaise or ketchup

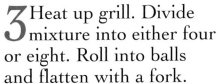

Barbie says:
No buns? Try shaping the mixture into sausage shapes around wooden skewers and grilling.

Dippy Chicken

Here's a fun and different way to eat chicken that the whole family will love, and there's a tasty peanut dip to serve, too! In the summer you could cook these on the barbecue for that extra special grilled flavor!

For 12 you will need . . .

For the marinade:

3 chicken breasts   1 tablespoon soy sauce   2 tablespoons honey   1 teaspoon mustard   1 tablespoon yogurt

For the peanut dip:

2 tablespoons warm water

2 tablespoons peanut butter   2 tablespoons brown sugar   1 tablespoon soy sauce

Barbie says:
Soak wooden skewers in water for an hour before using them to keep them from burning on the grill.

Cook's tools

Small saucepan   Tablespoon

    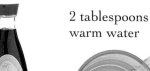

Sharp knife

Large mixing bowl   Wooden skewers   Chopping board   Wooden spoon

Finger Lickin' Chicken!

Serve your peanut dip in a pretty dish or saucer.

1 Using a sharp knife, carefully cut each chicken breast into four strips lengthwise (or more if they are large).

2 Measure the marinade ingredients into a large bowl and mix together well using a metal spoon.

3 Drop the chicken into the marinade and stir until each piece is well coated. Cover and refrigerate for one hour.

For a tangier taste, try adding a little garlic, ginger or chili sauce to the peanut dip!

4 Preheat grill. Thread chicken loosely onto skewers. Grill on top of stove or outdoor grill for five minutes, turning once.

5 Now make the peanut sauce. Put all the ingredients in pan on a low heat. Stir until well-mixed and warm.

Wooden skewers are sharp – always slide your Dippy Chicken off the skewer before you eat it.

Perfect Pasta!

Do you have a passion for pasta? Try my two favorite sauces — Tangy Tomato and Perfect Pesto. They're easy to make, delicious to eat, and look so sophisticated!

For 4 people you will need . . .

1 teaspoon olive oil

1 teaspoon salt

10 oz/250 g spaghetti or pasta shapes

For Perfect Pesto Sauce:

2 cloves garlic, peeled and crushed

2 oz /50 g Parmesan cheese, finely grated

2 cups/50 g fresh basil leaves

3 tablespoons pine nuts

½ cup/ 100 ml olive oil

Cook's tools

Blender

Measuring cup

Saucepan

Sharp knife

Chopping board

Tablespoon

Wooden spoon

Garlic mincer

Grater

Colander

To cook pasta or spaghetti:

1 *Boil* a large pan of water. Add salt and olive oil. Drop in pasta (if using spaghetti, push down with a spoon until it softens).

2 Cook according to instructions on the package, then taste a piece to see if it is done. Strain through a colander.

For Tangy Tomato Sauce:

1 carrot, *chopped*

1 stick celery, *chopped*

3 tablespoons tomato paste

14 oz/400 g can of tomatoes

1 clove garlic, peeled and crushed

⅔ cup/150 ml water

1 onion, *chopped*

1 tablespoon olive oil

Salt and pepper

For Perfect Pesto Sauce:

1 Put the garlic, basil leaves, pine nuts, and Parmesan cheese into a blender. You could also use a mortar and pestle.

2 *Blend* or pound until smooth, pouring the oil in gradually as you go.

Mix the pesto into pasta just before serving

For Tangy Tomato Sauce:

1 Heat the olive oil in a pan. Add onion, garlic, carrot, and celery. Cook for five minutes or until soft.

Pretty Pasta Colors!

2 Add tomatoes, purée, and water. *Simmer* for about 45 minutes, stirring every now and again.

Spaghetti or other ribbon pasta works well with either of the sauces

Barbie says:
To make your tomato sauce even more tasty you could add olives, capers, pepperoni, or a little chili sauce.

3 By now the sauce should be thick. Taste and add a little salt and pepper if you like.

Stuffed Baked Potatoes

Here's how to make an easy and delicious meal out of a potato! Baking them takes a long time so you'll have plenty of time to choose which tasty filling to put inside. Baked potatoes are good for you, too, but try to eat all the crunchy skin and don't add too much butter!

For 3 stuffed potatoes you will need . . .

3 large potatoes

1 tablespoon olive oil

Salt

For Cheesy Bean Filling you will need (per potato):

3 tablespoons baked beans, heated

2 tablespoons Cheddar cheese, grated

A few drops of Worcestershire or chili sauce

Salt and pepper

For Tasty Tuna Filling you will need (per potato):

2 tablespoons canned tuna fish

1 tablespoon canned corn

1 tablespoon mayonnaise

Salt and pepper

For Pepper Punch Crunch Filling you will need (per potato):

3 tablespoons cottage cheese

Salt and pepper

1 tablespoon raisins

½ a green and red pepper, *chopped* small

Cook's tools

Small mixing bowl

Sharp knife

Baking tin

Fork

Tablespoon

Chopping board

Sprinkle extra cheese on top!

Cheesy Bean Filling

1 Preheat the oven. Wash potatoes under running water. With a fork, prick each one several times.

2 Roll potatoes in olive oil on a baking pan. Sprinkle with salt and bake for 1 – 1½ hours.

3 Now make the filling. Simply mix all the ingredients together in a bowl and season. Chill.

Barbie says:
Take care when eating your baked potato. It's going to be Hot-Hot-Hot!

4 After one hour, test your potatoes. A sharp knife should slide in easily if they are done.

5 Using a sharp knife, make a cross in the top of each potato, and spoon in your filling!

For a special treat, put a little butter into your potato before the filling!

Pepper Punch Crunch Filling

Which is your favorite filling?

Tasty Tuna Filling

Nacho Nibbles

Having a sleepover is lots of fun, especially with a plate of Nacho Nibbles to share. There are so many things you can add to the recipe; they will taste deliciously different each time you make them — the only problem will be making enough for everyone!

For 2 to 4 people you will need . . .

Large bag of tortilla chips

2 tablespoons Cheddar cheese, grated

For the salsa:

1 small red onion, *chopped* finely

½ a 14 oz/ 400 g can tomatoes, sieved and *chopped*

Salt and pepper

1 teaspoon sugar

Pinch of chili powder (optional)

You could add any of the following toppings if you like:

Pepperoni slices

Olive slices

Pieces of green pepper

Cook's tools

Tablespoon

Wax paper

Chopping board

Small mixing bowl

Grater

Baking sheet

Fork

Sharp knife

Scissors

Teaspoon

First make the salsa: *Now put everything together:*

1 Preheat the oven. Put the tomatoes in a small bowl. Add the chopped onion and mix well.

2 Stir in the sugar, salt, pepper, and chili (if using). Mix everything together well and taste.

3 Now empty the bag of tortilla chips onto a baking sheet lined with wax paper and spread out.

It's **fun** to **Share!**

Barbie says:
You could serve your Nacho Nibbles with side dishes of guacamole or sour cream!

4 Spoon tomato salsa over chips, followed by any extra toppings you want to use.

5 Sprinkle the cheese on top and put in oven for five minutes, or until cheese has just melted.

Don't leave your Nacho Nibbles in the oven for too long or they will be too hot to eat!

Super Sundaes

The cool thing about sundaes is that you can make them with almost anything that's sweet and delicious. Surprise your friends with a sundae of their favorite fruits, cookies, or ice cream. Here are my favorite combinations for you to try. Which one do you like best?

A crisp wafer fan makes a classy addition to any sundae.

For a Fruity Sundae you will need . . .

2 tablespoons raspberries or strawberries

2 tablespoons *chopped* pineapple

2 tablespoons blueberries

½ a kiwi fruit, sliced

2 tablespoons vanilla yogurt

2 scoops strawberry or raspberry ice cream

Colored sprinkles

For a Chocolate Sundae you will need . . .

2 scoops chocolate ice cream

2 tablespoons mini marshmallows

1 small banana, sliced

Handful of mini cookies, or broken up big ones

1 tablespoon semisweet chocolate, grated

1 tablespoon toffee sauce

Cook's tools

Sharp knife

Tablespoon

Chopping board

Sundae glass

Ice cream scoop

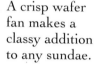

42

I wish it was sundae every day!

This pink icing flower makes my Fruity Sundae even more tempting.

1 First prepare your ingredients, then layer them in a pretty glass.

2 For a striking sundae, separate different colors and textures.

3 Top with a layer of ice cream or yogurt and decorate beautifully. Serve immediately!

A pretty glass is essential for a stylish sundae!

Barbie says:

Spoon some whipped cream on the top of your sundae for an extra special treat!

Best-ever Brownies

Here's a great idea for a sleepover treat! Brownies are easy to make and are delicious as a bedtime snack, with a glass of milk or juice. You could try adding pecans or walnuts instead of almonds — and white chocolate brownies taste really yummy, too. One is never enough!

To make about 15 brownies, you will need . . .

4 oz/100 g butter or margarine

2 eggs, *beaten*

1 cup/200 g brown sugar

2 oz/50 g bittersweet chocolate

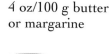

1 teaspoon baking powder

3 oz/75 g all-purpose flour, *sifted*

4 oz/100 g *chopped* almonds

Pinch of salt

Cook's tools

Medium saucepan

Wire cooling rack

Large ovenproof bowl

Spatula

Fork

Small mixing bowl

10 x 6 inch (25 x 15 cm) shallow rectangular cake pan

Wooden spoon

Pencil

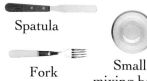

Sieve

Wax paper

1 Preheat oven. Grease pan well. Draw around base on wax paper. Cut out and place in bottom of pan.

2 Break chocolate into ovenproof bowl and melt with butter over a pan of *simmering* water.

3 Take bowl off the heat and add all the other ingredients. *Beat* well with a wooden spoon.

4 Pour the mixture into the lined cake pan and bake for 30 minutes or until firm to the touch.

5 Let brownies cool in pan before cutting into squares and transferring to a wire rack until cold.

Barbie says:
When you are melting the chocolate, try not to let the bowl touch the *simmering* water!

Brownies before bed!

Two Minute Treats!

These are the perfect treats if you are in a hurry, or are so hungry you just can't wait to dig into something delicious! Each recipe takes just a few minutes to prepare and even less time to eat!

Munch Mix

The perfect, healthy snack – great after school or while watching TV! Mix together two tablespoons of at least three of the following: nuts, sunflower seeds, raisins, dried fruit, or coconut.

Banana Booster Energy Sandwich

Feeling tired? Try this! Spread a piece of whole wheat bread with peanut butter and top with a sliced banana and another slice of bread.

Salad Snack Stop

Try this pretty mixture of flavors for a healthy snack! Combine shavings of Swiss cheese with seedless grapes, nuts, celery, and salad greens.

Popcorn Perfection

For a sweet sensation, melt a tablespoon of maple syrup and pour it over a bowl of popped corn. Sprinkle with a little cinnamon and eat right away, while it's still warm!

Ants on a Log

How's this for a creamy crunch with punch! Cut a piece of celery into 2 inch pieces. Fill hollow with cream cheese and sprinkle with raisins.

Fruity Floaters

For a delicious snack, make some pretty Fruity Floaters and sail away! Cut an apple into eight pieces and remove the core. Make triangles from cheese and fix them to the apple with toothpicks!

Creamy Dreams

Make hot chocolate according to package instructions. Top with hot frothy milk (use an electric hand mixer), or whipped cream, grated chocolate, and marshmallows. Creamy Dreams taste great with chopped nuts, and ice cream, too!

Fruity Fantasy

For four Fruity Fantasies, *blend* or use a fork to combine 10oz raspberries, one teaspoon lemon juice, 2 tablespoons sugar, ⅓ cup heavy cream, and 5oz fromage frais or sour cream. Serve in pretty dishes and decorate. Blackberry or Strawberry Fantasies taste great, too!

A Delicious Dip

Serve warm tortilla chips or colorful, crunchy vegetables with this: Mix three tablespoons sour cream with two tablespoons grated cheese and one tablespoon salsa (homemade, page 40, or from a jar). You could add lots of things to the sour cream and cheese mixture instead of salsa. Try a tablespoon of pesto (homemade, page 36, or from a jar) for a pretty, herby green dip.

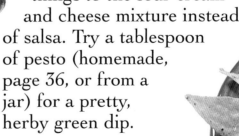

Barbie's Picture Helper

Sometimes recipes contain words or instructions that you might not understand. I hope this picture guide will help you with some of them.

Blending Mixing ingredients together in a blender until smooth. Don't overfill the container; always make sure the lid is on firmly, and ask an adult to help you!

Chopping Cutting into small pieces. For onions, peel and cut in half width-ways. With the flat side down on the board, make downward cuts. Now turn and make cuts at right angles.

Rubbing in Mixing butter or margarine into flour using just your fingertips (the coolest part of your hands) until the mixture looks like fine breadcrumbs.

Boiling Cooking something in water that is boiling (bubbling fiercely). **Simmering** Cooking something liquid over a low heat so it is bubbling gently, but not boiling.

Beating Stirring something really hard until it is smooth. Beat cake or cookie mixture with a wooden spoon and beat eggs with a fork.

Sifting Shaking flour or powdered sugar through a sieve to get rid of lumps and make it light and airy. Use a wooden spoon to help you.